Not a FAIRYTALE

Poems by Roxana Preciado

ISBN-10:1530855179
ISBN-13:978-1530855179

This book is dedicated to my family, my beautiful wife Marlene Preciado, and our amazing son Skylar Thomas Preciado. Without them I would be lost. Forever, I love you both.

PREFACE

At the age of 12, I started writing poetry as a coping mechanism to deal with my life challenges. I grew up in a family where my mother was often cold and distant. She was more of a guardian than an actual parent to me. I also had a stepfather and was the eldest of four siblings, me being the only stepchild to my stepfather. Needless to say, I was the black sheep of the family. Growing up, I had endured many trials and tribulations. I suffered from mental, physical and sexual abuse from those who were supposed to love and protect me the most. I found myself self-medicating with drugs and alcohol. By the age of 15, I was a drug addict. It was at age 16 when I told my mother I was gay. Instead of the warm and accepting embrace I was hoping for, my mother asked me to leave her home. I was left heartbroken and afraid. I had to figure out how I was going to survive on my own because I didn't have the help of my family. I was afraid to seek help from agencies and outsiders. I did not want to be put into the foster care system or even worse, for them to find out that I was undocumented.

I immigrated to this country at the age of 4 in 1989, and did not become a legal resident until 2014. I had to quickly come to terms with my limitations. I was underage, gay, undocumented, homeless and a drug addict. Life was anything but easy for me. I battled with depression for most of my life and had attempted suicide 3 times by age 18. I came very close to succeeding one of those times. I somehow found strength and motivation even in the midst of my despair. Writing was the light at the end of the tunnel for me, my only means of survival at the time. I have been diagnosed, misdiagnosed, and tried a variety of different forms of treatment. Unfortunately, none of these methods could "cure" me of "my condition." I have greatly healed and coped with my demons through the use of writing and painting. It is in my poetry that I have been able to record my story. It has been one of tragedy, endurance, and harsh realities.

Throughout all odds, I call myself today a survivor. I have succeeded! I stopped doing drugs at the age of 19 and made the decision that my past circumstance would not dictate my future. I worked hard to save money for my education and I am now more than ever determined to graduate with a bachelor's degree in the field of Psychology. I am only one year away from reaching this goal. I am married to an amazing woman and we have a beautiful child together. They represent everything I have ever wanted in a family. When I look back at the girl I used to be, it is hard to believe we are the same person. Though I am not ashamed of my past, I celebrate my beginnings because they have made me who I am today.

My story is detailed in my poetry throughout this book and it is my hope that I could help anyone who is facing similar hardships. To those struggling with their own obstacles, I would like to say to you: you will survive, you will succeed, you will be loved, and you are worth fighting for. I hope this book reaches those who need it, and to all others thank you for reading my story.

Mama, Mama

March 1998

Mama, mama

Do you love me? You are silent

You do not say

Mama, mama

Please say you do

Cause I'm in pain

& I love you

Mama, mama

What did I do?

I try my best just for you

Mama, mama

Now you say it, but I'm not there

It is too late

Mama, mama

I say good-bye

You try to tell me

But I am gone

Mama, mama

Now that I'm gone

Just remember

I died for your love

Never Again

1998

When my last tear has fallen and my eyes are but red

I will forget all the worry

I won't remember the pain

When my last tear has fallen, you will hurt me no longer

For this will be my last tear for us

 and I won't remember you

Ever again

Day by Day

July 1999

Never happy, never complete

Always crying, slowly dying

Day by day

Choosing to live blind and deaf

Careless and lonely as I am

Wanting to love, love itself

As willing to live as to die

Day by day

Wanting to forget dark haunting memories

Painful wounds that cannot heal

Losing myself in all my hate

Hurting more and more

Day by day

Sex

December 1999

You are my dream, my fantasy

I cannot touch just admire

But this desire is so impatient that no longer am I in power of my

body

It is so anxious to feel your touch

Your hands and body caressing me

all I can do is try to breathe

My lips ache to be relieved by a simple kiss

The passion so great

My lust for you

It cannot wait

Teenage Whore

December 1999

Everything and everyone keeps fucking me over & over again

Yet I welcome it

I continue to be a bastard of the world

My blood is poison

My heart is cold

My legs are open, ready to go

No longer my mother's daughter

I feel no pain, I feel no sorrow

I'm just a whore

Moonlight Escape

December 1999

I am dead

Yet still breathing

This lack of pain is so deceiving

And all these things I'm not believing

My heart is bitter and full of hate

Cause I have made many mistakes

My soul is blind

There is no light

I'll find escape coming tonight

I'm Yours

February 2000

8

Take me I'm yours

My lips are to kiss you

My arms are to hold you

And my soul is to love you

Hurt me I'm yours

My heart to break

My mind to play

And my body to use

Seduce me I'm yours

Hold me, kiss me, love me

And always remember

I'm yours

Dark Forces & LSD

July 2000

Fire at the pit of my stomach

Echoing screams coming from my room

Suicide thoughts running through my head

Sweaty palms aching to show my pain

My fast beating heart impatient to run away

Frustration driving me crazy

My body feels nothing but a rush of cold air and shadows everywhere

Voices that won't go away

Wounds that bleed to this day

Not healing

Not scarring, reopened each day

I'm trapped

Lost

Unable to get away

Hoping today is the last day

My last breath

Is this the end?

Every Other Teen

December 2000

Another day, another dead

Teen minds wondering into nothingness

Broken hearts, innocence lost

The media spreads the news

Another number… just another number

Was she more? Did the news let you know?

Spirits lost, wondered off to a land of love and acceptance

Not a worry or pain in the world

The scars she carries disappear

Self-inflicted wounds

Such a relief to know you are no more

To feel no pain the tears have stopped

Silence slowly replacing your dreams, memories, emotions

Her deep hidden secrets now nude to the world

Crushing her image, exploiting her thoughts

Another name for the yearly list

Another lost soul that could not let go

Buried, burned or other it's all the same

Forgotten

No more roses, no more tears

Once echoing screams now fading whispers

Another teen, another dead

Her story now lost with more current events

Who's Dreaming Now?

January 2001

A 16-year-old girl was found dead in her room. Her mom found her in the morning when she went to wake her up for school. In the girl's hand her mom found a note, and it read:

Dreaming so beautiful

Relaxing in heaven

Using the greatest

Guessing what's next

Seeing nothing but what you want to see

I found my heaven, my meaning, my life. I know I will not see another sunrise. I will not hear another wave. I will not taste anymore honey. I will not smell sweet apple pie. I will not feel the soft breezes on those warm sunny days. But I will dream. In fact, I'm dreaming, living in a more than perfect world. My reality is the only reality that exists for me. The whole world smiles at me and I laugh at the world. A second in my world extends to minutes, even hours of just complete bliss. A temporary perfect world and that is my heaven. I will not leave because it's all me. My soul belongs here in the land of everything that's beautiful. From here I will dream for everyone including you. Forever in my dreams.

A drug overdose and her mother just wants to know, if she is the one who is dreaming.

Predator

July 2002

There in the deep shadows I have found hope for tomorrow

I do not want tears, nor sorrows, nor fears

For now, I have died to be born once again

I'm better off now my bliss is so great

To hate and to hold

I have let everything go

I'm now cold inside, my black eyes cry no more

A bitch some will say

But even my kisses taste better than quality liquor

The poison I carry sinks deep in my heart

You yearn to be held and to be loved so much

A prey up ahead

I lure you to me and you beg me for more

Sin has never tasted so intoxicating before

Your soul you have lost in the shadows of lust

The wounded have died and I'm feeling great

Another has fallen in the pit of the world

I'm now once more empty

I must find another to fill me again

With the cover of night

I go hunt once again

Teenage Junkie

May 2003

It's been so long that my insides burn

My heart is racing, aching

Begging for it to bring me death

The forbidden bliss

My heaven on earth

The thought of it drives me crazy

Sick, I'll do anything to get it

I'm past insane

I'm fucking dying and in pain

I need a hit, just one more taste

The need

I need

I just can't breathe, I'm sick and weak

I seek the end in oblivion

When a junkie dies

No one cries

Questions

July 2003

Is this thing inside me a plague?

A thing that consumes me and kills me day by day?

Will writing help me breathe again?

Will tomorrow not bring the same again?

Could an angel share his wings to leave all this behind?

Or is it so, that I will never stop to cry?

What Now?

September 2003

What do you do when the world has turned its back on you?

What do you say when all you've ever said was not enough?

When all you feel is pain and mistrust

Should you just turn your back and let the past be that?

Or could you find a glimpse of hope in what you left behind

In those forgotten friends and long lost loves

In that family that just wasn't warm enough

In those long roads that you walked time and time again

Just to find yourself sad and lost again

Inside Me

January 2004

Today I rise from shattered glass, a broken past

I have peace at last

My shadows dim and my wings expand

Taking me places where angels dance

My inner child now freed at last

Where I feel no more pain or misery

You are no longer in my night dreams

Despite the falls and tricks you've conned

I flow and live in heaven's arms

The chain has broken and I have survived

The spoiled seed bloomed high and strong

Life didn't kill me after all

For I am beautiful and strong

Thanks to God I conquered all

Life Through Her Eyes

June 2004

"Young, bright, and beautiful" says the woman to me, as I finish the story of how I came to be. I explained how as a child I had to learn to keep hurt inside and smile. For if I didn't I might not make it through tomorrow. I told her how I found the power of my sexuality and how nothing in this life is free. I told her how I was forced to be a woman and sole care taker of me. I showed her the consequences of money and the price it had on me. Yet through it all she sat quietly and smiled at me. So I shared with her my secrets and what drove me to succeed. I explained my list of reasons, for each and every reason had deep meaning to me. That day I told her things I once promised myself never to repeat. Then when it was all over I said to me, "I am young, bright, and beautiful." Even if the only other person that knows why I am, what and who I am is the woman in me.

Diamonds

July 2004

I asked God for diamonds

Expecting to receive

Never really thinking, how fake diamonds look on me

I'm still a whore, a bitch, a cheat

The worst things I can be

It seems to ask for diamonds is a bit too much for me

Rush

June 2005

A life lived in the moment

Awaiting a clear breath

Still, I sit here in silence, too afraid to look or dare

My heart bound with secrets

My soul knows no exit doors

I just wait to see what may come

And hope I will survive it all

In Heaven

July 2005

22

Sincerely yours…

I write to her everyday

And though she won't reply to me

I love her anyway

My heart she hasn't yet returned

But I feel we'll meet again

To share another kiss

In heaven once again

Young Love

July 2005

What is true love?

Is it your worst pain?

Your greatest joy?

Or rather both

I accuse my heart of lying

Deceiving me everyday

I feel such joy and deep inside a regret

How could I be hurt this way?

If I thought I was in love again

My mind has run out of ideas

Of who is what, and what is who again

And since my heart's a liar

I'll ask my soul again

What is love?

Is it the pain that kills me?

Or the joy that wakes me every day?

Changes

September 2005

24

Heaven knows I've changed

If only in my heart

Still I breathe and walk the same

Yet my new life has begun

Touch Me

May 2006

25

Let me breathe from your kiss

Inhale your thoughts so that I can learn to read your heart

Let me seduce your soul so that we can make love in all the colors of

the world

Let me show you how a touch is beautiful & then embrace me

Let me, please let me

So that I can show you what it is to feel again

Once Upon A Time

June 2006

Touch me with your eyes

Undress me with a look

Remind me I'm a goddess

With the sweetest taste of honey

Kiss me with a smile

Embrace me with your lips

Let's explore the possibility

That this could finally be it

Passing

October 2006

27

Did you know I love me more?

I bet you never thought it possible, that I would love me insanely and

not you anymore

And yes I loved others while I still kissed you goodnight

Then when it came to ecstasy, I wasn't by your side

It wasn't really fair to say "forever mine"

In truth I knew, the moment I met you

That girls like you, are single layer and only passing through

Melissa

November 2006

28

If I gave you a seed would you plant it

And in that flower that bloomed would you see

All the different ways that I love you

And the many things that you mean to me

If in a box the stars I would give you

And the world was for just you and me

Would you believe that I really love you

Or think this was all just a dream

If I promise to make you immortal

If only in my memories

Would you fly to my heaven

And on a field of daisies

Would you make love to me

The Story

December 2006

I don't want to fight again

I fear if we speak, you will take the last breath from me

Who are you lover?

In the mist of all this chaos, I can't find that familiar face I laid in bed

with everyday

Am I the stranger?

Am I living a new life now, in a different time far from anything I

recognize?

Is it all over?

How do you know when it's the end, when the end is everyday

Is today a different day, a new beginning

A new life, a time far from ordinary

Am I not typical or regular?

I then must be extraordinary

Should we forget?

Can we forget, change the past, make up a happy ending?

A staged fabrication of you and me

A white lie with amazing lines and fictional characters

Our failed fairy tale dream

Take my hand again, this time not as your lover but as your guide

Explore deep inside me

Know I once was in love and high on you I flew

Never thinking twice or really thinking through, how much damage

you can do

I wish I could go back to the beginning

A place with infinite possibilities and in that second live forever

Let's stop time for you and me

Let's build a castle and in it my queen you will be

There, for you I will be whatever you may please

Flash forward to the truth, the black light

I never really lived this made up life of mine

We only played pretend, a game until the end

Now comes a new season

In the cold our petals lose their color and they fall

I don't want to fight again

We won't ever fight again

Liar

January 2007

In my head I hide many things

Locked thoughts, past events

I am a secret composed of many lies

Nothing true have people learned of me, I hardly exist

I drift through life a shadow

My lips pink and inside red with the desire

To just admit

I am a liar

Fein

February 2007

When you put your hands on me I tremble

I feel so anxious, I can't wait to kiss your lips

To look in your eyes and allow you to taste me

I want to get high on you

Feeling your skin against mine

Your warm deep breaths, you tremble like I

You have taken a piece of heaven

And engraved it all over my naked skin

Your fingerprints locked inside of me

Where no one else can see

And in that very moment I didn't need to breath

For you briefly made me an angel

You overwhelm me with all kinds of emotions when you flow all

over me

From my head to my feet, you caress and then embrace me

When I touch your body I can't help but get nervous

But not in fear of you

In fear of losing you

I give you my body and soul

And in your hands I become a sinner

Infatuated by you and all those little things you do

Ashamed I'm not, just astonished by what we do

And what your sweet words will make me do to you

There in the middle of lust and bliss

You have made me a Fein

Completely addicted to you

What else can I do but surrender to you

Swimming

March 2007

34

Out of all my time in this world, if I could rewind time to relive

another night it would be with you

The way you kissed, the smell of you, the ways of you

To live again in your eyes

I could see the birth of stars and understand the meaning of life

I want to see the oceans

So deep you said they went

I want to see your oceans, open for me again

Perfectly Complicated

March 2007

Living beneath your skin is helping me enter life

I can now see life with a clear view, through your eyes

There, I live my life now at the rhythm of your voice

Every day I live just a little bit more

When I am out, the sun cracks my skin

The world blows me in chaotic circles

With no rest areas for me to think

Luckily, your gravity pulls me towards you

And with a kiss, you put me back together

Build me better, to go back out into the world

For you, I'd climb an icy mountain to reach the books of truth

To finally understand, the inner workings of you

I want to swim in you

To feel just for a second, what it's like to be perfection

In you burns the desire to be the universe

With time expanding to forever

I want to be a star, a part of you

To maybe see you in your simplest form

Because you're so complicated

I, with my simple mammal mind

Cannot understand what it's like to be you

No Sleep

March 2007

Why can't I have you?

Is my scarred heart too much or not enough for you?

You're making me miserable

Can I play with you?

Spend a day with you?

I want to touch you

I memorized your name, your face, your bitchy ways

I want you to love me, take me, have me

Why can't I have you?

My palms are sweaty and I shake

I need a fix, give me a kiss

I want to lick your face

You taste almost like nothing

I want you to fill me with you

What is it about you that makes me want to die

Just to see you all the time

You're mean, I need you

I know I can never keep you

You're with so many people

Why can't I have you?

Why can't I have you!

Some Girl Marina

September 2007

I fucked her again

I laid her down in my bed again

It was hot so I bathed her

Made her a sandwich, while I drank the last of the now warm beer

I looked at her and felt nauseous

I was sickened by her aftertaste

I was sick

I wanted her again

She wasn't my only but she was my favorite

So I fucked her again

You Told Me

September 2007

You love it that I'm a pervert

You want me to teach you, hurt you, disarm you

You want to feel better

You need physical pain to quiet your emotions

A thrust of pleasurable hurt till numb

You tell me I'm wrong, sick, and just perfect for you

In lust and lost we feed on each other's desires

And destroy each other, till we need one another

You love it that I'm corrupted

You love girls like me

You're in pieces just like me

This Side Up

September 2007

Fragile you

What have I not done?

Sweet seed of my flower, how fragile are you

I carve you and mold you into perfect pieces of what I envisioned

Fragile you

How easy it is to make you divine

Tender piece of me, inside myself I keep all your memories in golden

files

Locked, safe, and kept away from any dust or shattering wind

Fragile you

I must confess, if I fail in my attempt with you

I will break

Happily Unhappy

October 2007

In darkness I think about losing you

I haven't yet had you but I cry and can't sleep because I've lost you

I'm happily unhappy

Always wanting what's not mine

It's you now, who lives in my dreams

You making me weak, I can't eat

My appetite reserved solely for you

I know if I had you, I'd no longer want you

I weep and weep

As I see you getting close to me

Oh, why must I have you!

I much rather want you

Dirty Laundry

November 2007

Sinning feels better when I do it with you

And for you, I will do anything

How about life, my life

What do you desire, please stay awhile

You smell of sweet mist

Your skin is pale, but when I touch it

Color covers every surface of your body

Am I delusional, or have I found faith in your face?

I've lost my last sleep

Your image haunting me, burying me in a sea of endless dreams

I am swimming in probabilities, waiting for you my sinner

Laid out in my lover's bed, wrapped up in our dirty sheets

Val

November 2007

I love those lips, those lips on you I do adore

Flushed with reddish pink and tasting so very sweet

Heavenly lips you carry and share with many

But only mean the world to me

Capture me in a spiritual dream of colors and patterns

I can never describe in words

Kiss me like no other, with those lips belonging to another

Surround me in a melody, composed by you and me

Let's rehearse with one another, every time we see each other

I love those lips, those lips on you I do adore

At times your lips are cold, they hurt my heart and soul

I cry and feel just like a child, frightened and alone

You scare me to the bone

I want to run away, regain my sanity

But I would miss those lips, I simply love those lips

Those lips on you I do adore

Kissing Girls

November 2007

45

I'm all kissed out now

My lips are numb from all my many lovers

My heart's been ripped to pieces and sewn up back together so many

times

I'm not quite sure it's even mine

I'm all cried out now

My eyes are dry and small from many nights of disappointment

And faking joy for one more

Imprinted on my cheeks are patterns of rundown mascara

Beneath my freshly painted skin

I'm all tired out now

I've been with you before

Just with another name and face and right before you came

You all just sound the same

I'm all kissed out now

If not a kiss, then what is it you seek in me?

In Truth

January 2008

Friend can we kiss again?

Twisted sick girl I want to hold your hand again

So sweet, so cute, so many things I want to do to you

I want to rip you open, just to bring you back to life

I want to take your sleep, I want to hurt you deep

Just to show you how much you mean to me

Doorbell rings 12am, and there you are again

Friend can we kiss again?

You taste much better when you're not my girlfriend

Attention Whore

January 2008

Leave me now, get out of my head

Stop your voice from choking my every breath

Fuck the day I met you, and fuck the day I kissed you

You said it was fate, I call it a mistake

Slut, whore, tramp, you sure like to think you're unique

Even I thought you were an angel, but I see now you're just a

stranger

I'm ashamed for you, everyone but me uses you

Even your leftovers are picked clean

There's nothing left of you for me

You've always loved the attention of anyone who is bored and

looking just to score

You're a washed up attention whore

Information Line

February 2008

What has the new day dust arranged for me?

I'm fighting hard, for something I'm not quite sure I really want

Unsatisfied moments and scraps of sinful smiles, accompany my fall

to greatness

Cheerful are my friends to see me yet again, blind and eager just like

them

Traveling with dangerous speed, unsettled destination

Expecting to be relieved and content with what I end up with

I wash myself clean and repeat my routine daily

I want to extract all the wine out of me

Wash away the smell of evening gatherings

Nights full of laughs and hazy pleasant times

But there is no time, the new night approaches

I'd rather lose myself in the buzz of the evening lights

I must get ready to get in line

Paint

February 2008

49

I want to cut you open and use your many shades of red

To paint a portrait of you, and show it to all my friends

I want to prove you're amazing and claim you as my new creation

I want to permanently have you

Beautiful face, I want you in perfect red

Blank

March 2008

Hiding in fear of humanity, I do not want them to hurt me

Living alone I begin to turn bitter and cold

Lying in bed I'm constantly busy locking away all my feelings

Paranoid, double checking there's no escape holes

I'm becoming antisocial and self-destructive but no one knows

Wondering around in my home, I try to pick up the phone

But who are all these people really?

To me, they seem like just a bunch of empty faces

Lacking depth and taking up spaces

Concrete cold, black hole deep

Am I truly looking for inner peace?

I feel as though I wasted today again

About Last Night

March 2008

51

Last night I went to bed with your fresh kisses on my lips

I didn't wipe them off, instead I licked them off... slowly

I love the taste of you in my mouth

I swallowed cautiously

I was afraid I might choke with the intensity of you

You asked, will I write about you

I said yes, because I was right about you

Field of Pretty Flowers

April 2008

52

Goodbye pretty girl

Don't forget to take your seeds as you go

I loved you and fucked you

I laughed and I cried with you

I'm done and I'm out

You're no longer what I obsess about

Goodbye pretty girl

I always knew I'd get bored of you

Girl with a Mission

May 2008

What you're missing I wish I possessed

What a disaster you came to create

Lost and obsessed

You fall for any poor schmuck who hands you a buck

Down again you go

Where you headed desperate girl?

Still seeking to be saved but you're almost at the end

There's little love left for cent out there

We've all become strangers to our neighbors

Friendship has now become part of the fiction section

Rumors of trust and unconditional love linger

With those old souls no one listens to anymore

The days of heaven coming again are folk tales

And you, so few like you

You with your love, passion, lust, heart

Those who dream as you do, are becoming like my mother

Extinct

Mad

May 2008

You've made me mean, angry, down

I'm mad at you

You have no shame or taste

I hate your favorite movie and pretty face

You've made me mean, angry, down

I'm mad at you

I hate your clothes and friends

They're annoying to no end

You've made me mean, angry, down

I'm mad at you

Your hair is lame

Just like the song you chose to dedicate that day

You've made me mean, angry, down

I'm mad at you

You walk so cocky

Yet, you still don't own that pair of socks you're always washing

You've made me mean, angry, down

I'm mad at you

You say you're deep, I think you're full

You're not artistic, you're a fanatic and only good at playing

interesting

And STILL you're bad at it

You've made me mean, angry, down

I'm just so mad

I'm just so mad about you

Working Girl

June 2008

56

In her head she lives daydreaming away

Front door basket child

Maybe your mother will open the door tomorrow

Her own body rejecting her, betraying her

Unbalanced and unpredictable

Will she smile or cry tomorrow?

To work…to work

If only she knew she's already there

Pet

July 2008

57

I'm your pet in a fishbowl but I can't swim

I beg and plead for you to free me

But you love to see me, you even feed me

You keep me alive just in case you might need me

Last Call

August 2008

Girls, girls, girls…press against the bathroom door

Locked together in between the dirty walls

Always wanting, grunting, moaning

Wishing to escape in each other's face

Living in clubs, bars, 'till last call

Trying to fill the empty with intoxication

Collecting moments that have become routine

To break the routine

They search the bottom of the glass for salvation and medication

Hoping to forget it all with another stranger

A flash of happiness and then

Blinding lights signaling the end

Reminding all the different colored souls they have to leave

and eagerly dream that the next night falls quickly

T-Shirt

August 2008

New shirt… the girls run to her

They wear her for a while and then dirty her

Leaving on her un-washable stains

Old new shirt

She has been thrown in the bottom of the laundry basket

No doubt she will soon be forgotten

She Is

October 2008

Intoxicating and vain

Seductive she turns her surroundings

Here she comes in those black heels stomping

Difficult and impulsive

A soul for your mind

She is THE woman, the wrong woman

She is dark light and she illuminates me

How I crave to penetrate that woman

Be that woman, my anonymous woman in colorful black

For her I'd give up what she lacks

A heart

Poet

October 2008

My tongue is drowning in words but I'm unable to release any

This script like life, fades me into the background

Next to everything else

I care nothing about

I'm left a poet without a heart

Lady Glass

October 2008

Broken skin, shattered heart

All behold the woman made of glass

She bleeds poison darts that penetrate your soul and self

'Till you've become someone else

She's the toxic in your lungs, the pain after a cut

She's the sleepless nights for the past few months

She travels in the moans and groans of all her shattered girls

She becomes immortal

Living in all who have fallen and now adore that heartless girl

She hides behind her scars

She lives in fear that one day the world will know the truth

That she is made of glass and weak

And she can be broken, just like you and me

Figure in my Mirror

October 2008

63

Figure, figure in my mirror, who are you today?

You possess infinite personalities and moods that shift in a blink

You swallow pills to make you laugh, pills to calm you down

Figure, figure in my mirror who will you become tomorrow?

They say you reside on the border but I disagree

Figure, figure in my mirror you don't seem borderline to me

You're so far gone not in between

Salty Fresh Water

November 2008

Existing, just being

Just being a human being

Alone, so alone

I cry, I crumble

I cowardly deny love to you, to all

Vain, vain your face is like champagne

Excruciating pain, such pain

Repetitive cycle, I wake everyday

One day closer, one less day

Broken into her father's lesson

Self-reliant her mother's gift

Once a child now a girl and deep within her, a woman soul

The world continues to spin, no one notices a thing

A life, alive, living, being

Breathing, just barely breathing

I want what I do not know

I persistently search for nothing at all

I have become the salt in the river we all know

In a Day

January 2009

66

In a day I lost the rest of my days

Every day after, all I thought of was that day

And today is a horrible day

Alley Cat

February 2009

Welcome home dirty cat

I see your claws need care and tending

You've been playing in the streets

Your fur is full of fleas and smells of rotting corpse

Dirty cat lay down for me, so I can groom you with my tongue

Clean and neat you leave again

Your fangs are sharp and need fresh flesh

Age is Just a Number

March 2009

I can't think clearly, I'm older and still I'm an infant

All decisions I make seem to lead to more mistakes

Wisdom comes with age, but what age is that?

I never seem to be old enough

The games of the world are no fun anymore

It's hard to be helpless and feel so alone

I don't get what's so great, about being clueless with age

Prescribed Smile

April 2009

Meds, meds, meds

Is it all just in my head?

Emotions running wild

I take one and disconnect them for a while

I feel not feeling any

I give generic smiles

I live my life on schedule

I take one then I smile

Sex, Water, Food

June 2009

Sex… what a delicious word

I can and do fuck who I please

I take the word SLUT and put it in my mouth, just to get it wet

Sex with her and her… I want all of them

Like eating, this too is a necessity

A necessity I love to fulfill

If it's wrong and sick, all the better that it is

I'm not a WHORE, I don't charge a cent

Instead I do it eagerly and willingly, I want it more than them

I'm not sick but I am savage

Will you let me, let it, let's have SEX

Light Packing

June 2009

My things, a table, chair

I leave behind

I leave behind

My bed and her sheets of memories

I do not care to take with me

My things all solid, pointless, empty things

I do not care to take with me

I leave behind

I leave behind

Paint on canvases all filled with my heart

These I have to keep, so I can breathe

My poems, notes, all with my soul I wrote

These I must keep so I can speak

All other things aren't really mine

I leave behind

I leave behind

I leave again

I always leave

I always leave, without a thing

Gay Girl

October 2009

Hate me because you envy me, envy my honesty

Fear me because I speak the truth, fear me because I know about you

Judge me because I'm happy, judge all that brings me joy

Strike me because you're angry, angry that I'm still standing

Art is No Coward

October 2009

74

Art, where the inappropriate is encouraged and celebrated

Art, a gateway to true freedom

Art, a reflection of a naked human being

Vicious And Lovely

January 2010

Is it your beauty?

Or that vicious way you decline my love

I've missed you very much

Your face, your voice, the feel of your heart and soul

My poet, my muse, my love how I've missed you

Stubborn loud distance that keeps you and I apart

When I think of you, I can't sleep or speak

Instead on those nights to you I write

To you forever I will write

Penny Lane

March 2010

What a slut! What a slut!

They say, but they're wrong

I'm not a slut, I'm a whore

I charge a pretty penny

I'm in the wrong lane, driving myself insane

Want to touch me?

Fuck me?

Have me?

I need to pay my rent

I'm Miss Penny Lane and I was born to be a whore

14 years old, "*Where you going young lady? ... Need a ride young*

lady?"

The predator said to me

A pedophile who confused me for a lady, but I was no lady

I may be young but to you I will never be a lady

I'll always be Miss Penny Lane

Getting money always starts with a penny

10pm

May 2010

Meet me at 9pm she said

Her voice like a dream

I could not believe it was HER

An hour in wait

My body shaking… I felt I would faint

I sneaked a few peeks and childishly I almost shrieked!

She still looked so sweet

At ten my life began yet again

At ten I had her in my arms again

Little Lost Child

May 2010

Little girl inside a massive, tragic, overload

Disappointed at the world

A hunger for acceptance

A desperation in her eyes

She just wants to fall in love, to be loved

But she never seems to get it right

Little foster child still searching for a home

Looking to finally have it all

A little girl who's always alone

When if ever, will she grow old?

The X

June 2010

79

The only way to kill her…

Is to cut off her head

Because her heart's made of metal

Authentic Crystal for a Princess

July 2010

My inner being's ego has been crushed

She loved her very much

My wails and screams so thick, they take over the sky

And make it want to cry

One day at a time

One day at a time

A step going nowhere

I know pain too well

A comfort in a way

My nest of abuse and neglect

A child stripped from innocence

A disturbed Cinderella

My rescuer never came

I never had a glass slipper

Instead I was handed a glass pipe

After a while, my heart was crystallized

So fragile it shattered

You stop being human when you lose your only given heart

A princess, I am not

Rachel Marie

August 2010

I hate you

I hate you

I hate you like I love you

Completely falling in the bottomless well

Well alone

 I'm alone

Pitch-black, in the dark I can clearly see

I see why

Why, why?

No excuses, only reasons

The reason is always me

I am the one who failed

Diluted blood, purple veins

Cold tears running down my face

Shrieking silence, torture

Your voice is dearly missed

A special occasion

You were my holiday

No matter what's today, I cannot celebrate

My skin is thin now, like cheap paper

Stories in me yet to be written on hold till you return

My crumbling pages

The death of a book

Halfway There

November 2010

84

Consume me life

Today I feel like giving up

Interior shattered, emotionally challenged

I am reaching the end of life

My youth is fading, I'm constantly failing

By choice I'm losing control

My sex drive is dead, my body's a mess

I refuse to pleasure myself

Torn, scraped, emptied

A piece of me is no longer there

I know I'll regret it

But today is not that day

Today is not that day

Girl Seeking Girl

December 2010

I'm addicted

Sex running loose

A look is all it took

Clothes dirty, hair greasy, fuck me eyes

No address, just a rage a need to feel

Impatient

A new kind of selfish

I knew right away I hated her

I wanted her

Society's trash

Thrown away because they all wanted her

They all wanted her to break

A goddess in the gutter

Wearing pretend as her evening dress

Stale red lipstick

Beneath all that makeup lies her true face

Glorious, taunting, haunting

Beautiful

Dirty lingerie, still warm from comfort sex

Ripping open her ridiculous costume

I badly needed all that's inside her

Every inch of her skin tastes like summer

Too many summers

She is hot to the touch

A fire fueled by her self-hatred

I melted in her mouth

Her tongue filled me with red wine

Drunk she helped me escape

I became someone else

Someone nothing like myself

We fucked and played pretend

In and out of bliss we floated

A crash of emotions

Sedated, liberated

Desperately doing it repeatedly

Sloppy at times but always starving

I couldn't leave

Silk tearing, it was wet and tainted

If ingested it would have killed me then

Now I Fein for it

An addict she left me

I never got her name but I can't forget her face

She disappeared into the bright LA lights

Where could she be tonight?

Identity Crisis

March 2011

Who is she supposed to be?

The artist

Painting with a knife all those pretty flowers

The poet

Whose pen she clings to

Afraid

Afraid as though it might leave too

The daughter

Successfully failing

She became the daughter her mother never wanted

The worker

Contemplating starving

Daydreaming of escaping

But she needs to fill her pockets

The student

Her head is filled with letters, numbers

Yet learning nothing that they taught her

The woman

Unevenly divided

She only knows, that no one knows about her

The wife

Bad at chores and candlelight

She wishes she was more of a 50's wife

The mother

Having a perfect child, son, companion

Trying her best to be what she always wanted

A mother

Who is she supposed to be?

Who am I supposed to be?

Pollination in the Summer

June 2011

I reach in me to see if I can find escape

You still my guide, absent of body

Your presence overtaking me

I feel you lover

I still feel for you my lover

Your hands that couldn't leave my every surface

I wish I was as brave as you

I would never have to choke on lies

Or play a tired role of wrong and right

I want to believe in fairytales

A romantic kiss under a summer tree

With all its leaves and purple flowers falling on you and me

A kiss and then

A thousand unanswered rhymes and questions

Too many to recall

Goodbye my summer lover

I'll write to you again

For now this is the end

My Many Guests

February 2013

92

Knitted dreams, unraveling

Apologies, damaged things

I'm fighting this battle inside of me

As the whole world watches me

A lot is at stake

If I fail I lose my sanity

Lust, sex, connection

I was nowhere in that equation

I lay my head on a soft bed and with every passing guest

I love myself less

I see why they want me

They see an empty place

And in this new and open place they will make camp

A fireplace for warmth and there will be water

Plenty of water

An anticipated adventure

In the wilderness

The animal with nothing but instinct can play

Grass with open flowers pollinating everywhere

Their seeds of emptiness sink deeper inside of me

Their hobby

Sweetness I beg, bitter my heart

Seduce my mind

Capture me and spread me out

Damage me into something nice

Deny me what I crave and need

Awake me from this horrid dream

Tonight I wait for my release

Again I cannot sleep

Instead I'll cum again

Maybe you'll be next

Dear Mother

February 2013

I never wanted to be bitter, bitter like her

I want to prove to her, I was no mistake

Show her that I can be loved and wanted

I was worth not throwing away that day

I'll be better next time mom

I swear I'll be better...

But I know I'll never be

No mother, no father

A child within a woman, now a mother

It's too late to be my mother

She rains affection on me on occasions

But my permanent umbrella prevents me from catching any

Divided, united in the fact that we each think we are right

I love you dear mother

But I will never be the daughter that you need

You took too much away from me

I am almost empty

You really broke me for others

I forgive you, I just can't forget

You will haunt me till the end

Death to a Flower

April 2013

Wilting flower you still smell of spring rain

Your once colorful petals, now are a crumbling gray

No sunshine for you and the air brought less and less

You used to be happy, I remember those days

Soft songs you would sing

To make the sun shine and smile at me

Then something, a force

Took all of your life

Drained you and left you to wither and die

Soon you won't breathe the sweet air anymore

They picked you too soon, they should have left you alone

I Wish I Was Rich

July 2014

I can hardly breathe…

I don't know if I deserve what I have

All my pretty things

I don't wish anymore, I just take and consume

I no longer have to cope, they say I have it all

I can't breathe…

I'm sick from too much caffeine I think

No one can comfort me

I am poor company

I see darkness in mid-summer days

My life just makes no sense

My peers envy my good fortune

But what they don't see, is the deep sadness inside of me

You just can't buy a new inner you

I'm not good enough

Not a good enough

Mother, lover, student, writer, artist, woman, lesbian

Not good at any of it

I'm too odd, too stressed, too weak, too me

No one seems to understand me

I have few friends and they never stay long

It must be me, I just know it's me

Money doesn't buy you anything worth keeping

Inside I will always be broke

I am broken

Storm is Almost Over

October 2014

99

Happiness has overtaken me completely

I feel so high and liberated

Life has given me a piece of peace

Finally, I am free and happy I am me

I Won't Cry When You're Gone

February 2015

I see the truth in your actions, your betrayal, my anger

It all left me anxious

I had enough, I took action

Said goodbye to your lying e-mail, text message

Pushed aside your treacherous displays of affection

I finally got the message

On the last day you came around, I saw your true form

Formerly mine, now I want you GONE

I now see what truly matters and honestly I missed me the most

You don't even get a goodbye from me

Instead I'll write you a poem, titled

"I Won't Cry When You're Gone"

Fuck Your Labels

September 2015

I want to be myself, just me

I want to forgive myself

Love me and all my many ME's

The bitch, the lesbian, the girl, the boy, the bi, the slut, the saint, the

sweet, the mean, the me

All of me

All of me is part of me, and every part is worthy of forgiveness

I just need to find the strength to be and forgive me

I want it so desperately

To forgive the lesbian

My mother's dreams of her little girl died with me

The girl

So complicated, emotional and weak

The boy

Heartless, cruel, detached from all but basic needs

The slut

Pleasuring me since I was 13

No boundaries, no morals, never saying no to me

She pleases me as she destroys me

The bi

Bisexual, homosexual, pansexual, queer, gay, me

All of me

I have so many versions of me

I can't keep track of the new label attached to me

I just want to accept me, forgive me, believe in me

JUST FUCKEN LOVE ME

I want to love me

Love me for me

Not a Writer

September 2015

Stripped from a verse of a love poem

You, you with all your sweet words

Letters, words, writing

How I love your writing

I write every night about you

My writer, a writer, your quotes all over my skin

In a sentence I was naked and in words you dressed me

Dressed me for you, I was covered with you

In your arms you touched more than my flesh

That day I left with a small part of you

Forever in the tip of my pen your essence will flow

My writer a writer, I wrote you a poem

Buildings in LA

October 2015

Creating a better version of me

I am under construction, and maybe over my head

Complex structure that crumbled with the weight of my past

Much work was needed but the blueprints have been found

The steel beams are solid now and have promise of greatness

I just hope I don't stumble

I'm afraid to collapse and perhaps never come back

Another LA building in the works

Another version of me will emerge

In a Girl

December 2015

In you my girl, a girl

Sweet sadness, my sad girl

A girl, two girls

Stumbling on empty dizzy speech

Can you pretend to rescue me?

Under balanced

Dirty walls

Half naked as they fall

Sloppy, savage, not quite ravaged

But who cares

They won't remember why tomorrow anyway

Crying at the end

The buzz of the evening lights has exhausted them

Rewritten

February 2016

I rose, I won

I vanquished my pain and destroyed my enemies

I did more than survive

I conquered

A warrior, a queen

A force

Feared

I have no more fear

Lessons learned, countless stories written

I will be remembered by those who thought they could kill my spirit

I am rewritten

They

February 2016

To be free I must surrender, give up

Let go of the world's image of me

What they say about me

To be happy I must rise above it all

I must take a look at what I have

Because that, that IS love

THEY ARE LOVE

Marlene

February 2016

A soulmate, my mate

Life

Our beautiful life

Life mates

Friend, lover, wife, mother

Family

You are my family

Completely, unconditionally, I will always be here

Loyalty and love, you'll never feel alone

I'll lead, I'll follow

But only by your side my love

Cheers to Happy Endings!

March 2015

I found her, she is…

Well… Amazing

Strong, smart, beautiful

She is the one

Believe me when I say I don't believe in fairy tales

Or soulmates, but she…

She's Amazing

I was empty when I lost her

It took me a century to admit it

I missed her

I am the one

I am my happy ending

Overcoming the worst of tragedies

And coming out of it all laughing

Smiling at it all because I won again

I want to say thank you to… well me

I can lift and rearrange the universe

I can do what suits me and right now the suit I wear is STRONG

Life is funny they say

Now that I've met you I believe it

You are funny

A minor side note in the story of me

Just minor, but you're funny

YOU'RE A JOKE

My mother locked up in her head

There in her made-up world, she can live with herself

She's alive but only one of us is living

My father… a true villain

Yet I'm here

The damage so deep it could only be reached and repaired by me

I fixed me… I fixed ME

You know what's funny?

The power of perception

Homeless, hungry, drug addicted teenager

Or in the words of my favorite teacher Mr. Flores,

"Smart, kindhearted, hardworking honor student, such a good girl

that one"

The power of perception

18-year-old undressing for strangers, to survive on her own

All the while, dreaming of going to college

In her possession, a box full of rolls of dollars

Undocumented, AB-540, no fingerprints

Dreamer… you will succeed

In my dreams the whole world whispered survive to me

Happiness…

I finally have her…and him

Her, him, wife, son

FAMILY

I have a family

I went from walking and looking at the cracks on the concrete floor

To sitting outside just to look up at the sky

Blue, white, clear…

BEAUTIFUL

Life is beautiful

Wrapped up so deep in them, it's like being in my mother's womb

again

Fairy tale complete with villains, but villains never win

In my happy ending

YOU JUST DON'T EXIST

THE END

Made in the USA
Monee, IL
07 July 2026